English

Age 6-7

Contents

Activities

Quick Tests

Lynn Hug **ouis Fidge**

Speaking and listening (1) – descriptions

It is important to be able to describe and explain things clearly – because then people understand what you mean!

1 **Describe your family to a friend.**

a Talk about how big your family is.

b Talk about where members of your family live.

c Talk about the jobs that the grown-ups do.

d Describe the things that your family likes to do.

e Draw a picture of your family in the box.

2 **Describe your favourite toy.**

a What is your favourite toy? _____

b Why is it your favourite? _____

c What does it look like? _____

d What does it do? _____

e How do you play with it? _____

f Draw a picture of the toy on a piece of paper to show when you are giving your explanation.

Speaking and listening (2) – explanations

It is important that you can describe and explain things clearly to other people – because then they will know exactly what you mean!

1 Do you have a pet? If not, find out about a pet you would like to own. Use the questions below to make some notes that explain to a grown-up how to take care of your pet.

a What equipment does your pet need?

b What does it eat?

c Where does it sleep?

d What exercise does it need?

e What toys can it play with?

f Draw a picture of your pet on a piece of paper that you can show when you are giving your explanation.

2 Imagine you are teaching a friend how to draw a picture of a house with a garden. Use the questions below to make notes about all the steps they need to follow.

a What equipment do they need?

b What do they draw first? Why?

c What comes next?

d How do they draw windows?

e What will go in the garden?

f Draw a picture of a house on a piece of paper to help you explain.

dge and ge

The letter strings *dge* and *ge* sound very similar – but they are spelt differently.

ba**dge**

bagga**ge**

1 Finish the words by writing *dge* or *ge*.

a bri**dge**

b ima**ge**

c villa**ge**

d nu**dge**

e sta**ge**

f ju**dge**

g ra**ge**

2 Choose the correct *dge* or *ge* word from the box to complete each sentence.

> package   lodge   edge   dodge   fridge   page   fudge

a This __fudge__ is delicious!

b We are staying in a wooden __lodge__ for our holiday.

c I have finished the last __Page__ of my book.

d I got a __pakege__ from Nana for my birthday.

e It fell off the __edge__ of the table.

f There is juice in the __frige__.

g I had to __dodge__ the ball!

__Samreen H__

4

kn and gn

The letters *kn* and *gn* go at the start of a word. They both sound like *n* because the *k* or *g* is usually silent.

knee

gnome

1 Complete the words by adding the correct letters: *kn* or *gn*. Then draw a line to match each word to the correct picture.

a _____ kn ot

b _____ kn itting

c _____ gn ome

d _____ kn ife

e _____ at

f _____ kn ight

g _____ uckle

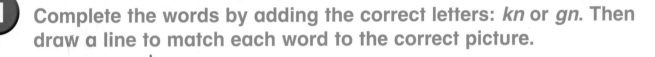
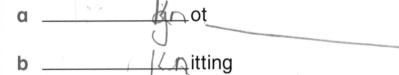

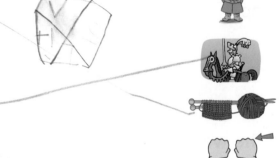

2 Circle the correct spelling of each word and cross out the incorrect word. Write a sentence using each word.

a (knock) gnock _____

b knaw gnaw _____

c (know) gnow _____

d knash gnash _____

e knu gnu _____

wr

Some words start with the letter pattern *wr*. When you say it out loud, you only hear the sound *r* because the *w* is silent.

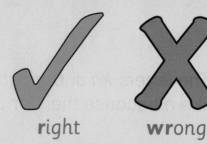

right   wrong

1 Complete the words by adding the letters *wr*. Then draw a line to match each word to the correct picture.

a ___wr___eck

b ___wr___ite

c ___wr___ist

d ___wr___inkle

e ___wr___ap

f ___wr___eath

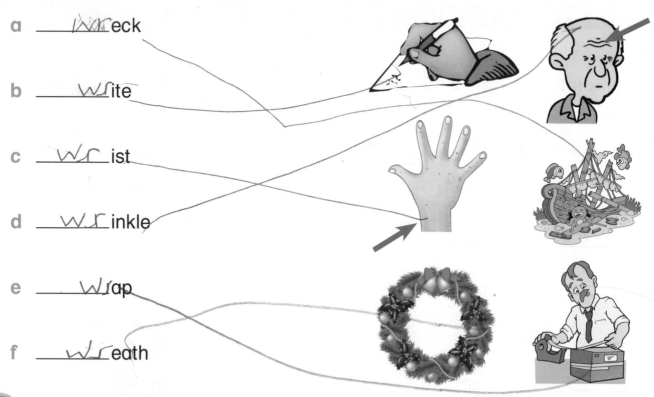

2 Find all the words that start with *wr*. Colour in the boxes, then write the words below.

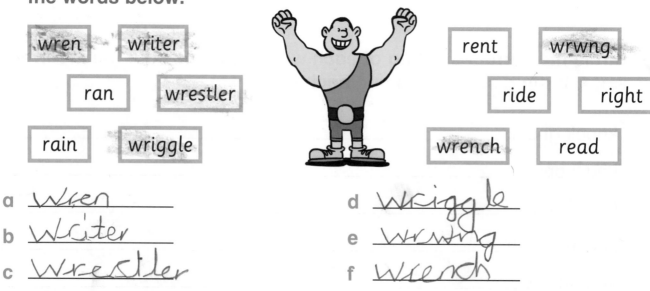

wren	writer
ran	wrestler
rain	wriggle

rent	wrwng
ride	right
wrench	read

a ___wren___

b ___writer___

c ___wrestler___

d ___wriggle___

e ___wrwng___

f ___wrench___

6

al and *il*

The word endings *al* and *il* sound very alike.

festiv**al**

pup**il**

---

1 Learn these spellings using the LOOK, COVER, WRITE, CHECK method.

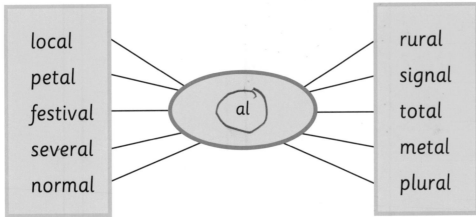

local
petal
festival
several
normal

al

rural
signal
total
metal
plural

---

2 Choose the correct ending by adding *al* or *il* to finish these words.

a pup_il_

b tot_al_

c civ_al_

d penc_il_

e met_al_

f sign_al_

g ev_il_

h foss_al_

1000
10
1000

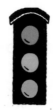

le and *el*

The *le* and *el* endings sound the same. The best way to know the difference is to learn the spellings. Remember to use the LOOK, COVER, WRITE, CHECK method.

easel

bott**le**

---

1 Complete the words by adding *le* or *el*. Then choose three of the words and draw them in the boxes. Label your pictures.

a eag**el**

b tunn**le**

c map**el**

d ang**le**

e simp**le**

f hot**el**

g litt**le**

h gigg**le**

i chap**el**

---

2 Underline the correct spelling of the word to complete each sentence. Cross out the incorrect spelling.

a I would like a **doubel double** choc chip ice cream, please.

b Just turn the **handel handle** and open the door.

c I saw a **squirrel squirrle** in the park.

d I went on a minibeast hunt and found a worm and a **beetle beetel**.

e I went to the **castel castle** and saw suits of armour.

f I washed my face with a **flannel flannle**.

g Please change the television **channle channel**.

Spelling *y* and *ies*

Here is a spelling rule for words that end in a consonant plus *y*. When you make the word plural (more than one), you change the *y* to *ies*.

baby

bab**ies**

1 **Change these words to the plural.**

a sky  _____

b country ➡ _____

c berry ➡ _____

d body ➡ _____

e spy ➡ _____

f jelly ➡ _____

g lady ➡ _____

h study ➡ _____

2 **Now change these plurals to the singular (one).**

a parties ➡ _____

b ponies ➡ _____

c puppies ➡ _____

d stories ➡ _____

e enemies ➡ _____

f cities ➡ _____

g cherries ➡ _____

h flies ➡ _____

3 **Label the pictures. Be careful – is it singular or plural?**

_____ _____ _____

wh and *ch* blends

Lots of words start with the sounds *wh* and *ch*.

whiskers

cheese

1 Write in the missing letters *wh* or *ch* to complete the words.

a ___Wh_ale

b _____imp

c ___Wh_isk

d ___ch_air

e ___Wh_iteboard

f ___ch_ips

g ___ch_illy

h ___Wh_eat

i ___Wh_istle

2 Write a word beginning with *wh* to complete each question.

| When | Who | What | Why | Which | Where |

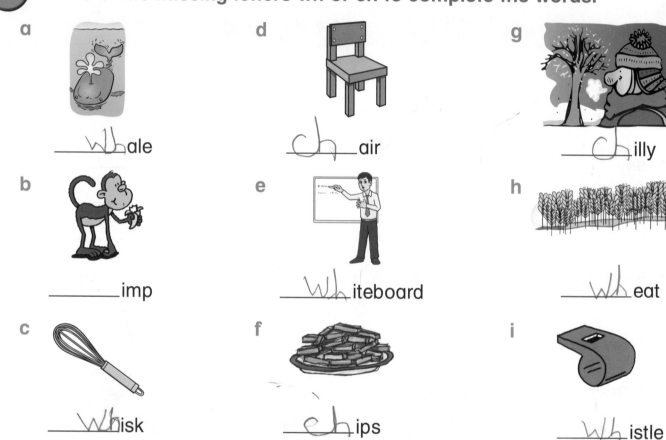

a ___What___ do you want to eat for lunch?

b ___who___ lives at number 7 Willow Street?

c ___wirch___ book do you prefer?

d ___where___ are you hiding behind the sofa?

Suffixes

Change the *y* to *i* before adding a suffix that starts with a consonant.

empty + ness = emptiness

Drop the *e* at the end of a word before adding *ing, ed, er, est* and *y*.

wide + er = wider

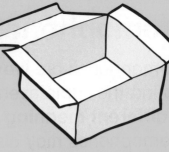

---

1 **Add the suffix to each word.**

a beauty + ful = ___beatiful___

b lonely + ness = ___lonliness___

c happy + ly = ___happly___

2 **Add the suffix to each word.**

a hike + ing = ___hike + ing___

b shine + y = _____

c nice + est = _____

Sun + Shine = S

Look out for one syllable words that end with a single vowel followed by a single consonant. Double the last letter when you add ing, ed, er, est and y.

pat + ing = patting

3 **Add the suffix to these words.**

a hum + ing = _____   d fat + er = _____

b drop + ed = _____   e run + y = _____

c sad + est = _____

Homophones

Homophones are words that sound the same even if they have a **different meaning** or **spelling**. Homophones may also be spelt the same, such as *bear* (animal) and *bear* (carry or put up with).

An example would be:

two *the number 2*
too *as well*
to *as in going to*

1 Draw a line to match the pairs of homophones. The first one is done for you.

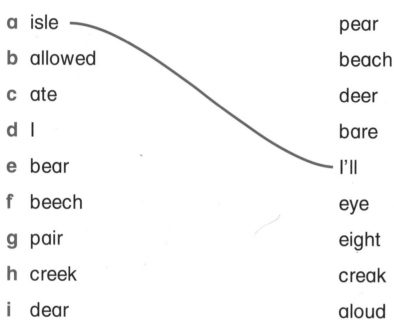

a	isle	pear
b	allowed	beach
c	ate	deer
d	I	bare
e	bear	I'll
f	beech	eye
g	pair	eight
h	creek	creak
i	dear	aloud

2 Cross out the homophone in each sentence that does not make sense.

a My auntie said I had **grown groan** since she last saw me.

b My **hare hair** is blonde.

c Can I come **two too**?

d A **herd heard** of sheep ran towards me.

e The **hole whole** class said hello.

f **Our Hour** cat likes fish.

g I **know no** your name.

h I **moan mown** if I have toothache.

Contractions

When you change a word to its shorter form, it is called a contraction. You use an **apostrophe** to show that one or more letters are missing.

it is ⟶ **it's**

1 **Draw a line to match each pair of words to its contraction.**

a   can not   won't

b   will not   isn't

c   is not   I'm

d   do not   can't

e   I am   couldn't

f   I would   I'll

g   I will   don't

h   could not   I'd

2 **Choose the correct contraction from the box to complete each sentence.**

I'll	I'd	she's	It's	can't	don't	didn't

a   ___I'd___ like to fly to the moon.

b   This sum is too hard. I ___can't___ do it.

c   When I get back from holiday ___I'll___ come and see you.

d   Jessica lives next door and ___she's___ my best friend.

e   Come to DisneyWorld! ___it's___ fantastic.

f   Why ___didn't___ you come to school yesterday?

g   I ___don't___ like chips so I never eat them.

Words ending in *tion*

The ending *tion* is said 'shun'. Learning this letter pattern will help you to spell lots of longer words.

frac**tion**

po**tion**

---

1 **Fill in the missing letters.**

a audi t i o n

b celebra t i o n

c cau t i o n

d collec t i o n

e reflec t i o n

f infec t i o n

g rota t i o n

h suc t i o n

i hiberna t i o n

j tradi t i o n

---

2 **Choose a word from the box to complete each sentence so it makes sense.**

| tuition   station   fiction   exhibition   action   operation   auction |

a I bought an antique vase at the _exhibition_

b I have music _tuition_ to help me play
   the violin.

c My gran went into hospital for an _operation_ to
   make her better.

d I caught a train at the _station_.

e I like _action_ films, where lots happens.

f I like reading _fiction_ better than non-fiction.

g I saw some great art at the _exhibition_

Possessive apostrophes

Possessive apostrophes show **ownership**. With singular words, you just add *'s* to show ownership.

If the word is plural and ends in s, the apostrophe comes after the *s*.

The cat**'s** whiskers. | The cat**s'** whiskers.

1 Add the possessive apostrophe in the correct place.
All these are singular.

a   The dogs paws were cold.

b   The girls shoes were red.

c   The mans hat blew away!

d   The horses mane is long.

e   The boys lunch was tasty.

f   The womans bag was heavy.

g   The babys cry was really loud!

bad baby

2 Now add the possessive apostrophes in these sentences.
All these are plural.

a   The dogs tails were all wagging.

b   All the girls books were about the seaside.

c   The birds beaks were pecking at the peanuts.

d   The puppies paws were so tiny!

e   All the cats bowls were empty.

f   The bats wings were flapping.

g   The boys coats were warm.

Statements, questions and exclamations

You get clues about whether sentences are statements, questions or exclamations. Statements have a **full stop** at the end, questions have a **question mark** and exclamations end with an **exclamation mark**.

. ? !

1 Question or exclamation? Write Q or E in the box.

a I love chocolate cake! [Q]

b Is it time for tea yet? [E]

c What is your name? [ ]

d That was loud! [ ]

e I was really scared! [ ]

f Would you like a biscuit? [ ]

2 Statement, question or exclamation? Write S, Q or E in the box.

a I went shopping for new shoes. [ ]

b That's my favourite show too! [ ]

c Can I have a drink, please? [ ]

d What is your favourite game? [ ]

e I had cereal for breakfast. [ ]

f Is that your dog? [ ]

Commas in a list

When you make a list of things in a sentence, you should **separate** them with commas and put the word *and* between the last two things on the list.

I bought some eggs, potatoes, carrots, bananas and peppers.

1 **Add commas in the correct places for each sentence.**

a I like cats dogs and rabbits.

b I read books comics and newspapers.

c My favourite foods are cake toast and oranges.

d I collected shells stones and seaweed to decorate my sandcastle.

e Rainbows are red orange yellow green blue indigo and violet.

f It is cold so put on a hat scarf and gloves.

g I drink orange juice cola and milk.

h I saw tigers lions and hippos at the zoo.

2 **Write sentences about these things. Include lists and don't forget the commas.**

a animals _____

b games _____

c clothes _____

d toys _____

e vegetables _____

f plants _____

g bugs _____

h sports _____

Questions

Question marks show when a question has been asked.

Are we there yet**?**

Special question words also give us clues that questions are being asked:

Why Where
When What
Who Which How

1 Add the question marks to these sentences.

a What is your name__

b "Can I come too__"
asked Mary.

c Why can't I__That's not fair!

d Would you like a sweet__

e Why not__ I want to!

f Do you like snakes__

g Do you want to come with me__ I don't mind.

h Can we go today__

i Who was that__

j Would anyone like some supper__

2 Choose a word from the box to make each question make sense. You can use the words more than once.

Why	Where	When	What	Who

a _____ said that?

b _____ are my keys?

c _____ is your name?

d _____ did you do that?

e _____ time is it?

f _____ is my pen?

g _____ can we go to the park?

h _____ would like to play with me

i _____ shall we go shopping?

j _____ would you like to drink?

Alphabetical order

Do you know the alphabet? Things are often organised in alphabetical order, so it is a good thing to know.

1 Write these words in alphabetical order.

a dog, cat, elephant

cat elephan dog ✗

b cake, pie, sandwich

cake pei sandwich

c pear, apple, orange

pear orang apple ✗

d child, toddler, baby

child baby toddler ✗

e plate, cup, spoon

cup spoon plate ✗

2 Now write these names in alphabetical order.

a Lucy, Ben, Peter

Ben Peter Lucy ✗

b Selma, Nora, Jake

Nora Selma Jake ✗

c Rajan, Tom, Alex

Tom Alex Rajan

d Marissa, Charlie, Pat

Charlie Marisa Pat

e Nicholas, Lena, Sophia

Nicholas Sophia Lena

Breaking words down

When you spell words, it is useful to break them into **smaller chunks**. This helps when you are reading too.

Drawing could be easily broken into dr-aw-ing.

1 Break these words into small chunks. Then learn to spell them.

a	**snail**	breaks down into	sna - il
b	**writing**	breaks down into	writ - ing
c	**hotel**	breaks down into	ho - tel
d	**maybe**	breaks down into	may - be
e	**donkey**	breaks down into	donk - ey
f	**flowers**	breaks down into	flow - ers
g	**carrot**	breaks down into	car - ot
h	**important**	breaks down into	po - rt - tant
i	**computer**	breaks down into	com - pul - ter

2 Write the missing chunks of each word. Use the words in the box to help you.

because
brother
sister
window
animal
should
jumping
another

a sh-ou-ld

b br-oth-er

c be-cau-se

d win-dow

e an-i-mal

f Ju-um-ping

g sis-ter

h an-other

Verbs

Verbs are the action words in a sentence. They tell you what is being done. Some people call them '**doing words**'.

Lick is a verb. It tells us what is being done.

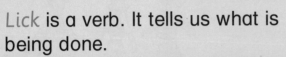

1 Underline the verb in each sentence.

a The bird flew away.

b The girl laughed at her brothers.

c The mother ate a big slice of cake.

d The snake slid across the rocks.

e The lion roared.

f The two brothers shouted very loudly!

g The mouse squeaked as it ran.

h The sun shone brightly.

i I ran down the street.

2 Complete each sentence with a verb that makes sense. Use the verbs in the box to help you.

a The giraffe ___ate___ leaves from high branches.

b The dog ___Barked___ at the postman.

c My dad ___Snores___ very loudly!

d The teacher ___Wrote___ her name on the board.

e The spider ___Lurked___ in the corner.

f The horse ___galloped___ away.

g The cat ___Pured___ because it was happy.

h The waves ___Rea___ up the beach.

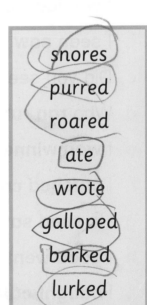

snores
purred
roared
ate
wrote
galloped
barked
lurked

Tenses

The words we write tell us whether things are happening now, in the past or in the future.

I am walking is the **present** – now.

I walked   is in the **past**.

I shall walk   is in the **future**.

---

1 Write whether these sentences are in the past, present or future tense.

a   I sat on the chair.   _____

b   I went to the party.   _____

c   I'll see you in the morning.   _____

d   She saw a cat.   _____

e   I shall go to school tomorrow.   _____

f   I am laughing.   _____

g   I can see a rainbow!   _____

h   I ran all the way home.   _____

i   I am reading a great story.   _____

j   I am swimming.   _____

2 Cross out the incorrect verb in each sentence.

a   I **wented went** to school today.

b   I **seen saw** a whale!

c   Did you **see saw** that sunset?

d   Who **ran runned** the fastest?

e   I **won winned** the race!

f   I **catched caught** the ball.

g   He **seed saw** the film today.

h   I **goed went** to my Granny's yesterday.

i   I **caught catched** a cold.

Compound words

Compound words are made from smaller words **joined together**, without changing the spelling.

butter + fly = butterfly

1 Draw a line to match the parts of the compound words to make new words. The first one is done for you.

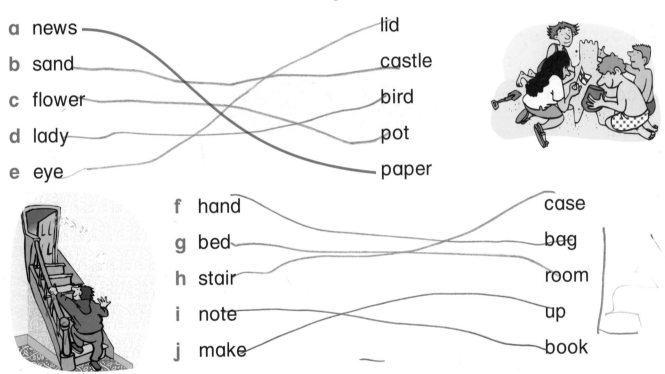

a news   lid
b sand   castle
c flower   bird
d lady   pot
e eye   paper

f hand   case
g bed   bag
h stair   room
i note   up
j make   book

2 Use the words in the box to make 10 compound words.

| ball crow fish board stick day bull skate stack week |

a scare _crow_

b _skate_ board

c star _fish_

d cup _board_

e hay _stack_

f birth _day_

g _bully_ dog

h lip _stick_

i _week_ end

j foot _ball_

Syllables

Syllables are the **chunks of sound** that make up words. If you say words out loud, you can hear the syllables.

bathroom has two syllables:

bath + room

crocodile has three syllables:

croc + o + dile

1 Count the syllables in each word. Then write the answer in the box.

a caterpillar [2]

b leaf [ ]

c garden [ ]

d rainbow [ ]

e spider [ ]

f butterfly [ ]

g ladybird [ ]

h bird [ ]

i hedgehog [ ]

j greenhouse [ ]

2 Rewrite the words in order, with the word with the lowest number of syllables first.

a daisy rose buttercup _____ _____ _____

b chinchilla cat rabbit _____ _____ _____

c planet sun universe _____ _____ _____

d sausages eggs bacon _____ _____ _____

e orange banana lime _____ _____ _____

f pen pencil computer _____ _____ _____

g telephone mobile talk _____ _____ _____

h tea chocolate coffee _____ _____ _____

i sandwiches cake trifle _____ _____ _____

j scorpion ant beetle _____ _____ _____

Suffix *ful*

The letters *ful* can be added to the end of words as a suffix. When you add the suffix *ful* to a word, you are saying that it is **full of** something.

A spoon**ful** of sugar is a spoon **full of** sugar.

1 Write new words using the suffix *ful*.

a Full of hope [hope + ful] = ✓ *hope ful*

b Full of joy [joy + ful] = ✓ *Joyful*

c Full of peace [peace + ful] = ✓ *Peaceful*

d Full of sorrow [sorrow + ful] = ✓ *sorrowful*

e Full of colour [colour + ful] = *colourful*

f Full of doubt [doubt + ful] = *doubtful*

g Full of cheer [cheer + ful] = *cheerful*

h Full of power [power + ful] = *Powerful*

i Full of thought [thought + ful] = *thoughtful*

2 Write the meaning of each word. If you don't know, use a dictionary.

a wonderful *means that you love to enjoy*

b playful

c useful

d helpful

e hopeful

f joyful

g truthful

h beautiful

i hateful

25

Suffix *ly*

In this sentence, the word *carefully* is an adverb. It tells **how** the girl made the model. The *ly* at the end is a suffix, added to the word *careful*. By adding *ly* we make an adverb that tells us how something happens or is done.

The girl made the model plane **carefully**.

1 Complete each sentence with the correct adverb from the box.

| happily | kindly | lazily | delicately | roughly | selfishly | sadly |

a The boy _Kindly_ shared his sweets.

b The cat stretched out _Lazily_ on the chair.

c My grandma smiled _delicate_ when she saw me coming.

d The man frowned _Selfishly_.

e The butterfly fluttered _happily_ from flower to flower.

f The boy _Sadly_ said he would not share his toys.

g The swimmer rubbed herself _roughly_ with the towel.

2 Draw a line to match each adverb to the correct description.

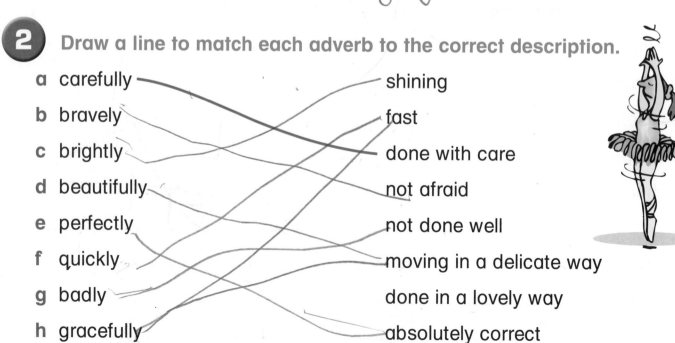

a carefully   shining

b bravely   fast

c brightly   done with care

d beautifully   not afraid

e perfectly   not done well

f quickly   moving in a delicate way

g badly   done in a lovely way

h gracefully   absolutely correct

Suffixes *ment*, *ness*, *less*

Suffixes can be added to words to make new words.

The suffix *ment* can be added to pave to make pavement.

The suffix *ness* can be added to full to make fullness.

The suffix *less* can be added to time to make timeless.

1 Add the suffix to each word.

a base + ment = _Basement_

b weight + less = _Weightless_

c bad + ness = _badness_

d end + less = _endless_

e cheerful + ness = _Cheerfullness_

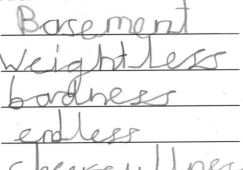

2 Draw a line to match each word to the correct suffix.

a move — ment

b bashful — ness

c enjoy — ment

d agree — less

e age — ment

Tricky spellings

Some words do not seem to follow spelling rules or are difficult to work out by saying them out loud. You just have to learn them by heart.

every   *gnat*   *neither*

1 Learn these tricky words using the LOOK, COVER, WRITE, CHECK method.

a only   *only*

b little   *little*

c down   *down*

d their   *their*

e because   *because*

f could   *Could*

g would   *Would*

h should   *Should*

i does   *does*

j goes   *goes*

2 Spend a few minutes looking at each word. Cover it up. Then try to write it from memory. Check your spelling against the original.

a mother   *mother*

b father   *farther*

c always   *allway*

d once   *once*

e upon   *upon*

f after   *aftar*

g every   *every*

h eight   *eight*

i brother   *brother*

j before   *before*

28

Writing stories (1) – plotting

Plotting a story is fun! You get to think about all of the exciting things that will happen in your story.

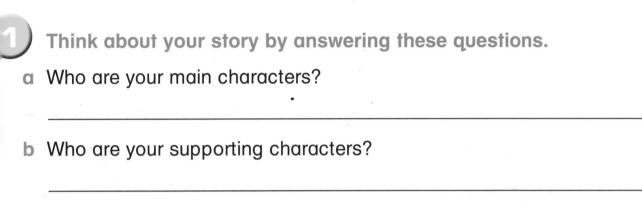

1 Think about your story by answering these questions.

a Who are your main characters?

_____

b Who are your supporting characters?

_____

c Where is your story set?

_____

d Will you use the weather to help to build the atmosphere?

_____

2 Now think about the action of your story.

a How will your story start? A good beginning will make your reader want to read the whole story, so make it exciting!

_____

b Is there a 'main event' in the story?

_____

c What is the main problem to be solved?

_____

d Think of a good, strong ending.

_____

Writing stories (2) – characters

Once you have a plot line, you need to start thinking about your characters. They are what bring your story to life!

1 Answer these questions about your main character to help you.

a What is your character's name?

_____

b What does your character look like?

_____

c What sort of clothes does your character wear? Does that give the reader hints about the sort of person they are?

_____

d What is your character's voice like?

_____

e What is your character's hair like?

_____

2 Now answer these questions to develop your character further.

a Where does your character live?

_____

b Does your character have any habits?

_____

c Does your character have a job?

_____

Writing shape poems

Shape poems are written in the shape of the subject of the poem. The subject is the main thing that the poem is about.

1 Write a cloud poem. You can use some of the words in the box. Write your poem around the cloud outline.

The sky is beautiful
The birds flew

drip	mist
drift	drizzle
damp	float
dark	grey
deluge	pouring

2 Now write a flower poem. Make a list of words to use. Then write your poem around the flower outline.

_____

_____

_____

_____

_____

_____

Test 1 **Adverbs**

Adverbs tell you **how**, **when** or **where** action takes place.

Millie eats her
dinner **greedily**.

Mum is **always**
busy.

We like to play
outdoors.

1 Circle the adverb in each pair of words.

1. (quickly)   quick

2. (slowly)   slow

3. noisy   (noisily)

4. often   cats

5. cake   never

6. nearby   jumped

7. ran   later

8. (happily)   can

9. nice   (cheerfully)

10. (completely)   sad

10
9
8
7
6
5
4
3
2
1

Colour in your score.

Test 2 **Adjectives**

Adjectives **describe** nouns.

The **shiny red** ladybird crawled along the leaf.

Underline the adjective in each sentence.

1. The big dog ran away.

2. The little mouse squeaked.

3. The tall man laughed loudly.

4. The tiny baby giggled quietly.

5. The long snake slithered across the ground.

6. The golden sun shone brightly.

7. The hairy spider scuttled up the wall.

8. The old woman wrote a letter.

9. The furry rabbit jumped high.

10. The brown worm wriggled under the leaves.

Colour in your score.

33

Test 3 Word order

We have to write words in the **correct order** so they make **sense**.

eat Monkeys bananas. ☒

Monkeys eat bananas. ☑

Write these sentences correctly.

1. milk. Cats drink   *Cat drink milk*

2. lay eggs. Birds   *Birds lay eggs.*

3. asleep. is dog The   *The dog was asleep.*

4. balloon A pop. can   *A bloon can pop.*

5. is The green. grass   _____

6. A hop. frog can   _____

7. red. My is coat best   _____

8. swim pool. You a in   _____

9. wash a You sink. in   _____

10. tree tall. very The is   _____

Colour in your score.

34

Test 4 **Adding *ing* and *ed***

We can add *ing* and *ed* to the end of some words.

Yesterday I walk**ed** to school.

Today I am walk**ing** to the shops.

Write these words so they end in *ing*.
Spell them correctly.

1. miss   *missing*

2. shop   *shoping*

3. write   *writeing*

4. carry   *carring*

5. crash   *crashing*

Write these words so they end in *ed*.
Spell them correctly.

6. beg   *beged*

7. blame   *blamed*

8. copy   *copyed*

9. splash   *splashed*

10. rub   *rubbed*

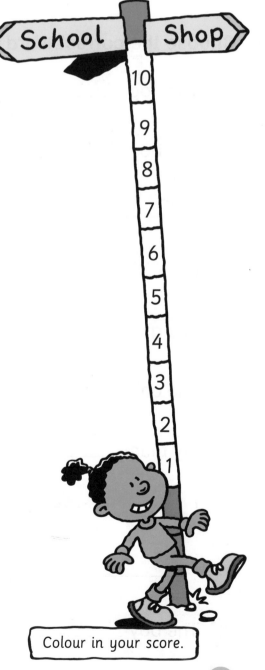

School   Shop

10
9
8
7
6
5
4
3
2
1

Colour in your score.

Test 5 Making sense of sentences

Sentences must **make sense** when you read them.

The aeroplane **flied** in the sky. ☒

The aeroplane **flew** in the sky. ☑

Choose the correct word to finish each sentence.

1. The dog _bited_ the postman. (bit/bited)

2. The boy _broke_ the window. (breaked/broke)

3. I _catch_ the ball. (catched/caught)

4. I _saw_ the moon. (seed/saw)

5. The girl _is_ reading. (is/are)

6. The children _were_ running. (was/were)

7. My mum _came_ home. (come/came)

8. I _went_ in the shop. (went/goed)

9. I _have_ got an apple. (has/have)

10. The boy _hurted_ himself. (hurt/hurted)

Colour in your score.

Test 6 Conjunctions

A conjunction is a **joining** word. It may be used to join **two sentences** together.

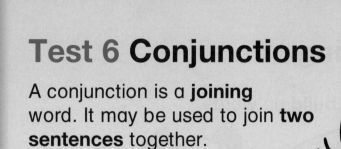

EEK

A mouse is small. An elephant is big.

A mouse is small **but** an elephant is big.

Choose the conjunction *and* or *but* to fill each gap.

1. I picked up the apple _and_ ate it.

2. The girl found her bag _but_ went to school.

3. I got the sum right _and_ Ben didn't.

4. The lion stopped _and_ roared.

5. I like swimming _but_ reading.

6. I sat down _and_ watched TV.

7. This door is open _but_ that door is shut.

8. Metal is hard _but_ wool is soft.

9. I got undressed _and_ went to bed.

10. I opened my bag _and_ took out a book.

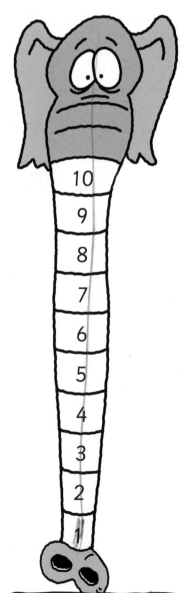

10
9
8
7
6
5
4
3
2
1

Colour in your score.

Test 7 Word building

In spelling we have to learn to **build** up words.

h + ow + l = howl

Do these sums. Write the words you make.

1. l + ou + d = _____

2. d + ow + n = _____

3. m + ou + th = _____

4. f + ou + nd = _____

5. cr + ow + d = _____

6. cl + ow + n = _____

7. sh + ou + t = _____

8. sp + ou + t = _____

9. fl + ow + er = _____

10. cr + ou + ch = _____

Colour in your score.

38

Test 8 Full stops and question marks

I live in a house.

Where do you live?

A **sentence** often ends with a **full stop**.

A **question** always ends with a **question mark**.

Rewrite each sentence correctly. Add capital letters, full stops and question marks in the correct places.

1. a farmer lives on a farm _____

2. why are you late _____

3. bees live in a hive _____

4. what is the matter _____

5. where is my pen _____

6. the fox ran quickly _____

7. the clouds were black _____

8. who is your friend _____

9. the wind is blowing _____

10. how did you do it _____

Colour in your score.

39

Test 9 Compound words

Compound words are made up of **two smaller words** joined together.

lady   +   bird   =   ladybird

Do the word sums and write the answers.

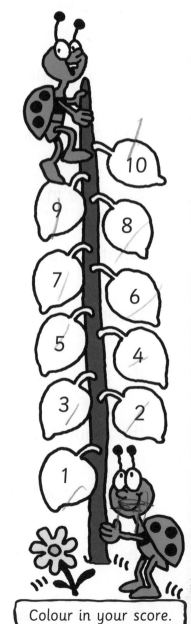

1. foot + ball = *fooball*

2. rain + bow = *raibow*

3. sun + shine = *sunshine*

4. snow + man = *snowman*

5. play + time = *playtime*

6. butter + fly = *butterfly*

7. bull + dog = *bulldog*

8. hedge + hog = _____

9. black + berry = _____

10. key + hole = _____

Colour in your score.

40

Test 10 Playing with words

You should always look for **patterns** and **similar spellings** in words – it helps you to learn to spell new words!

cake

rake   shake   lake

Write the new words you make.

1. Change the **f** in **f**air to **ch**.   Lace

2. Change the **r** in **r**are to **fl**.   _____

3. Change the **t** in **t**ear to **b**.   _____

4. Change the **l** in **l**ord to **c**.   _____

5. Change the **j** in **j**aw to **cl**.   _____

6. Change the **c** in **c**ore to **sh**.   _____

7. Change the **w** in **w**ire to **f**.   _____

8. Change the **p** in **p**ure to **c**.   _____

9. Change the **f** in **f**ind to **w**.   _____

10. Change the **r** in **r**oar to **s**.   _____

Colour in your score.

41

Test 11 Speech marks

Speech marks, or inverted commas, show someone is **speaking**.
We write everything the person says **inside** the speech marks.

I deliver letters.

The postman said,

"I deliver letters."

Put in the missing speech marks.

1. The builder said, I use a hammer.

2. The driver said, I drive a big lorry.

3. I am feeling tired, said Mrs Smith.

4. The librarian said, I work in a library.

5. The farmer said, I keep cows on my farm.

6. The queen said, I wear a crown.

7. The nurse said, I work in a hospital.

8. My job is dangerous, said the firefighter.

9. The caretaker said, I keep the school clean.

10. I make bread, said the baker.

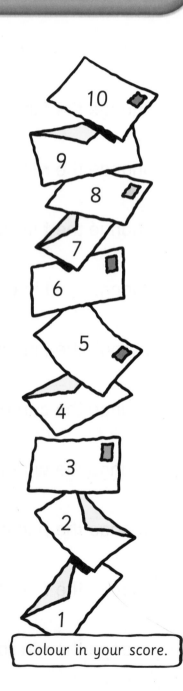

Colour in your score.

Test 12 What's going on?

All of these verbs (action words) describe **actions** that are going on in the past or present tense. Notice that they all end in *ing*.

Choose a verb from the box to complete each sentence. Think carefully about your answers to make sure every sentence makes sense.

crying	swimming	sitting	flying	sleeping
laughing	running	barking	baking	walking

1. I was _Swimming_ fast. _laughing_

2. She is _____ slowly.

3. Mum was _____ down.

4. The dog was _____ fiercely.

5. The fish is _____ through the weeds.

6. A butterfly was _____ from flower to flower.

7. Nana was _____ my favourite cake.

8. My cat Layla was _____ in the sunshine.

9. Dad is _____ at a funny programme.

10. The baby was _____ so I picked her up.

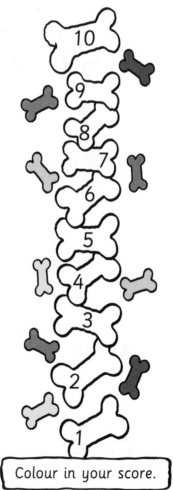

Colour in your score.

43

Test 13 **Verbs**

Verbs tell us what someone is **doing**.

MOO!

A cow **moos**.

Choose the best verb to complete each sentence.

moos   clucks   purrs   neighs   hoots
squeaks   gobbles   bleats   quacks   barks

1. A cow <u>moos</u>.

6. A horse _____.

2. An owl _____.

7. A dog _____.

3. A hen _____.

8. A sheep _____.

4. A duck _____.

9. A mouse _____.

5. A turkey _____.

10. A cat _____.

10
9
8
7
6
5
4
3
2
1

Colour in your score.

44

Test 14 Checking your work

Always check your writing to see if you have made any silly mistakes.

goes
The rocket ~~go~~ fast.

Write the correct word to complete each sentence.

1. My uncle _Is_ very nice. (is/are)

2. The birds _were_ very noisy. (was/were)

3. The children _are_ reading. (is/are)

4. The girl _were_ asleep. (was/were)

5. The cat _lickes_ milk. (like/likes)

6. I _did_ it well. (did/does)

7. My cousin _came_ to visit. (comed/came)

8. I _tore_ my shirt. (teared/tore)

9. Tom always _tries_ hard at maths. (try/tries)

10. Lions _Roars_. (roar/roars)

Colour in your score.

45

Test 15 Expanded noun phrases

You can make your writing more interesting by expanding noun phrases. A phrase is a **collection of words.**

The cat meowed. ➡ The **velvety black** cat meowed.

Make these sentences more exciting by expanding the noun phrases with descriptions.

1. The _____ frog croaked.

2. A _____ dog barked.

3. The _____ sun shone.

4. The _____ spider scuttled away.

5. A _____ dolphin swam past.

6. The _____ stars twinkled.

7. The _____ monster sang.

8. Some _____ hopped away.

9. A _____ lion roared.

10. The _____ teacher was cross.

10
9
8
7
6
5
4
3
2
1

Colour in your score.

Test 16 Commas

Commas are used to **separate** things in a **list**.
We **don't** use a comma before the word *and.*

sheep, duck, donkey and hen

Fill in the missing commas.

1. red yellow blue and green

2. lion tiger cheetah and leopard

3. apples pears bananas and grapes

4. pen pencil crayon and felt-tip

5. rain sun snow and fog

6. I saw a car a bus a lorry and a bike.

7. In my bag I took a mirror a ruler and
   a pencil.

8. I like oranges peaches cherries and
   melons.

9. I can play football cricket rugby and
   snooker.

10. A gardener needs a spade a fork a
    trowel and a hoe.

Colour in your score.

Test 17 Adding to the end of words

Sometimes we can change words by **adding letters** to the **end** of them.

The kitten likes to **play**. It is very play**ful**.

When *full* comes at the end of a word we spell it *ful*.

Do these word sums. Write the answers.

1. use + ful = *useful*

2. hope + ful = *hopeful*

3. help + ful = *helpful*

4. pain + ful = *painful*

5. beauty + ful = *beautiful*

Take off *ful*. Write the word you are left with.

6. colourful ___ *Colour* ___

7. faithful ___ *faith* ___

8. truthful _____

9. cheerful _____

10. plentiful _____

how are you ?

10
9
8
7
6
5
4
3
2
1

Colour in your score.

48

Test 18 Questions

A question should begin with a **capital letter** and end with a **question mark**.

What is this**?**

Rewrite each question correctly.

1. who looks after our teeth

2. what flies in the sky

3. where is your shirt

4. what do we use to dig with

5. who lives next door to you

6. where do we get milk from

7. why are you crying

8. how did you do that

9. who is your best friend

10. what makes a seed grow

Colour in your score.

Test 19 Exclamation marks

We use an **exclamation mark** when we feel **strongly** about something.

What a mess!

Rewrite each sentence. End each sentence with either a question mark or an exclamation mark.

1. come quickly   *Come quickly!*

2. who are you ?   *Who are you?*

3. when did you arrive ?   *When did you ~~arrive~~*

4. stop messing about   _____

5. what a nice surprise   _____

6. what are you doing   _____

7. you are horrible   _____

8. this cake tastes good   _____

9. why are you so upset   _____

10. shut that door   _____

Colour in your score.

10 9 8 7 6 5 4 3 2 1

50

Test 20 Singular and plural

Singular means **one** thing. Plural means **more than one** thing.

Excaple

one sweet   lots of sweets

Complete the phrases.

1. one rabbit, lots of _rabbits_

2. one chocolate, lots of _Chockla_

3. one wish, lots of _____

4. one cap, lots of _____

5. one pony, lots of _____

6. one _____ , lots of plates

7. one _____ , lots of horses

8. one _____ , lots of boxes

9. one _____ , lots of rockets

10. one _____ , lots of fairies

Colour in your score.

51

Test 21 Capital letters

We use a capital letter to **begin** the names of **people**, the names of **days of the week** and **months of the year**.

My name is **S**hanaz.

My birthday is in **M**arch.

Write and spell correctly the name of some months.

The name of the months begining with *J*.

1. January   2. July

3. June

The name of the months ending with *ber*.

4. November   5. October

6. December   7. september

The name of the months begining with *A*.

8. August   9. April

The name of the month begining with *F*.

10. February

Colour in your score.

Test 22 Writing about real events

Writing about real life events is like being a newspaper reporter!

Write about an exciting day out. Answer the questions in full sentences.

1. Where did you go?

   _____

2. What time of year was it?

   _____

3. What was the weather like?

   _____

4. How did you travel?

   _____

5. What activities did you do?

   _____

6. What did you have for lunch?

   _____

7. Were there any special treats or snacks?

   _____

8. Did you see anything unusual?

   _____

9. Did you learn anything new?

   _____

10. Did you buy anything, such as a souvenir?

   _____

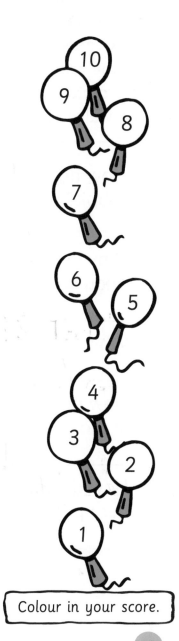

Colour in your score.

Test 23 Open ended questions

Open ended questions do not have one 'correct' answer – they want your views.

Read this story and answer the questions.

The door of the hutch swung open. The fox was waiting, and it chased the rabbit through the fence, out of the garden and into the open field. Jenny saw from her bedroom window, and she ran down the stairs. She shouted at the fox and leapt over the gate, chasing it. The rabbit hid in the bushes, and the fox tried to force its way in through the brambles.

"I'm coming, Flopsy!" Jenny called. "You go away, horrible fox!" As she got closer, the fox looked at her and ran a few steps backwards, and then it crept back towards the bushes, looking for the rabbit. Jenny waved her arms, and with a last look the fox ran away. Jenny crawled into the bushes and caught Flopsy, stroking her as she walked back to the house. "You are safe now," she said.

1. How do you think Jenny felt when she first saw the fox chasing the rabbit?

   she felt su horrible

2. Why do you think the fox took a few steps backwards when it was shouted at?

   He took a few steps back because he was startled

3. Why do you think Jenny waved her arms?

   Because she wanted the rabbit to notice her

4. How do you think Flopsy felt when she was hiding in the bushes?

   She felt scared and probably petrified

5. How do you think Flopsy felt when Jenny picked her up and stroked her?

   She felt relived

Colour in your score.

54

Test 24 Comprehension (1) – instructions

Instructions tell you what to do, so it is important that you can understand them.

Read these instructions for making pizza and answer the questions.

What to do:

1. Slice the mushrooms.
2. Spread the puree on the pizza base.
3. Add the mushrooms.
4. Grate the cheese and sprinkle on the top.
5. Sprinkle herbs over everything.
6. Bake the pizza in the oven until the cheese is slightly browned.

You need:

pizza base

tomato puree

cheddar cheese

mushrooms

herbs

1. Name three of the pizza ingredients.

   Tomato, chedder and herbs.

2. What do you do with the mushrooms first?

   You slice the mushrooms.

3. How do you prepare the cheddar cheese?

   Grate the cheese and sprinkle on top.

4. What do you sprinkle on the pizza after the cheese, before baking?

   Sprinkle herbs

5. How do you know when the pizza is ready?

   You can tell when the cheese is slightly browned.

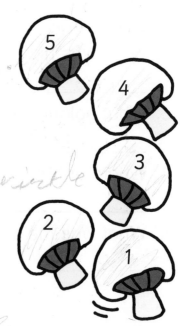

Colour in your score.

Test 25 Comprehension (2) – dialogue

Dialogue gives a reader lots of information, so it is important that you can understand what is being said.

Read the dialogue and answer the questions.

"I loved that film! The scary queen was brilliant!"
"She was great. I really liked her spiky crown. I liked the purple dragon best though."
"The castle looked brilliant – especially the giant spiders in the dungeon."
"I thought the spiders were terrifying!"
"Oh yes – and that ghost hiding in the woods – very scary!"
"I really jumped when it popped out of the tree stump!"
"I nearly fell off my chair! I dropped some popcorn."

1. Where were the spiders?
   In the dungaen.   Woods.

2. What was hiding in the woods?
   That ghost war hiding in the

3. What colour was the dragon?
   Purple

4. Where did the ghost pop out of?
   It poped out the tree stump

5. What was the queen's crown like?
   Spiky.

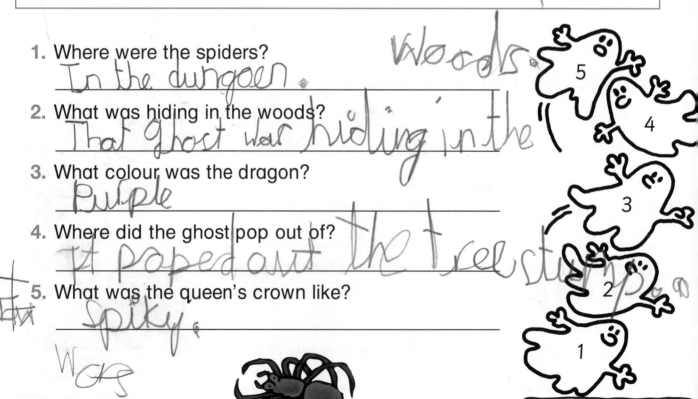

Colour in your score.

Comprehension exercises help you to see if you understand what you have read.

Read this passage and answer the questions.

Ladybirds are marvellous beetles. There are over 5000 species in the world and 46 species in Britain. They smell with their feet and produce smelly liquid from their knees to warn off predators. They can fly at speeds up to 15 miles per hour and flap their wings an amazing 85 times each second!

1. How many species of ladybirds are there in Britain?

   _5000_

2. What part of their bodies do ladybirds use to smell things?

   _their feet and produ___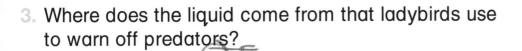

3. Where does the liquid come from that ladybirds use to warn off predators?

   _85_

4. What speed can ladybirds fly at?

   85 time at speed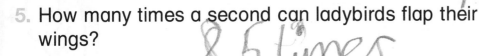

5. How many times a second can ladybirds flap their wings?

   8 6 times

Colour in your score.

Test 27 Comprehension (4) – traditional tales

Comprehension questions about a traditional tale can help you to see if you have really understood what you have read.

Read this part of a story and answer the questions.

Goldilocks was walking in the forest when she saw a cosy cottage in a clearing. As she knocked on the door, it creaked open, so she went inside.
In the kitchen, she could smell a delicious, creamy smell. Her tummy rumbled. Three bowls were sitting on the table. Goldilocks rushed across the room, and popped a spoon into the first bowl of porridge. She scooped up a blob of porridge and stuffed it in her mouth.
"Ew! Too cold!" she cried. She saw a second bowl of porridge and tried again.
"Ow! Too hot!" she yelped. She saw a third bowl of porridge and tried again.
"Oh yum!" she smiled. "Delicious – it's just right!"

1. Where was Goldilocks walking?

   She was forest

2. What did she see in a clearing?

   Cottage

3. What could she smell in the kitchen?

   Some porridge

4. What was wrong with the first bowl of porridge?

   to hot

5. What did she think of the last bowl of porridge?

   fine

5
4
3
2
1

Colour in your score.

Test 28 Comprehension (5) – fictional narrative

Comprehension questions about a story help you to see if you have understood what you have read.

Read this story and answer the questions.

The mermaid hid in the kelp forest. She felt the tiny fish tickling her as they slipped backwards and forwards round her tail. She could see the dolphin searching for her under rocks and in piles of shells, and she giggled to herself. A passing seal winked at her as he rushed towards the surface.

1. Who was hiding in the kelp?

   The Mermaid

2. What tickled her tail?

   A Fish

3. Who was looking for her?

   Some seal dolphin

4. What creature winked at the mermaid?

   Seal

5. Where was the seal going?

   Surface

5

4

3

2

1

Colour in your score.

Test 29 Writing *ai, ar, un*

It is important to practise your handwriting so that people can read all the good things you write about!

ai   ar   un

Write these *ai, ar* and *un* words. Use your best joined-up handwriting.

1. chair _chair_

2. train _____

3. drain _____

4. fairy _____

5. bark _____

6. shark _____

7. start _____

8. bun _____

9. fun _____

10. under _____

Colour in your score.

60

Test 30 **Writing *ab, ul, it***

Some handwriting patterns are difficult, because they join a small letter to a tall letter.

ab ul it

Write these *ab, ul* and *it* words. Use your best joined-up handwriting.

1. about   *about*

2. baby   *ba*

3. table   _____

4. rabbit   _____

5. pull   _____

6. bull   _____

7. full   _____

8. bit   _____

9. bite   _____

10. hit   _____

Colour in your score.

61

ANSWERS

Page 2

1. **a** A description of the size of your child's family (sisters, brothers, cousins, etc.)
   b A description of where family members live (adult siblings, grandparents, parents, etc.)
   c A discussion of jobs that adults in the family do, if any
   d A discussion of things the family enjoys doing
   e A picture of the family

2. Your child should describe their favourite toy – what it is like, why it is the favourite, how it is played with, etc.

Page 3

1. Your child should answer the questions about their pet – or the pet they would like to have.

2. Your child should explain how to draw a house.

Page 4

1. **a** bridge   **e** stage
   b image   **f** judge
   c village   **g** rage
   d nudge

2. **a** fudge   **e** edge
   b lodge   **f** fridge
   c page   **g** dodge
   d package

Page 5

1. Make sure your child has drawn a line to match each word to its picture.
   a knot   **e** gnat
   b knitting   **f** knight
   c gnome   **g** knuckle
   d knife

2. Any sentences which make sense.
   a knock   **d** gnash
   b gnaw   **e** gnu
   c know

Page 6

1. Make sure your child has drawn a line to match each word to its picture.
   a wreck
   b write
   c wrist
   d wrinkle
   e wrap
   f wreath

2. wren, writer, wrestler, wriggle, wrong, wrench

Page 7

1. Make sure your child has learnt the correct spellings.

2. **a** pupil   **e** metal
   b total   **f** signal
   c civil   **g** evil
   d pencil   **h** fossil

Page 8

1. **a** eagle   **f** hotel
   b tunnel   **g** little
   c maple   **h** giggle
   d angel/angle   **i** chapel
   e simple

2. **a** double   **e** castle
   b handle   **f** flannel
   c squirrel   **g** channel
   d beetle

Page 9

1. **a** skies   **e** spies
   b countries   **f** jellies
   c berries   **g** ladies
   d bodies   **h** studies

2. **a** party   **e** enemy
   b pony   **f** city
   c puppy   **g** cherry
   d story   **h** fly

3. puppies, jelly, cherries

Page 10

1. **a** whale   **f** chips
   b chimp   **g** chilly
   c whisk   **h** wheat
   d chair   **i** whistle
   e whiteboard

2. **a** What   **c** Which
   b Who   **d** Why

Page 11

1. **a** beautiful
   b loneliness
   c happily

2. **a** hiking
   b shiny
   c nicest

3. **a** humming   **d** fatter
   b dropped   **e** runny
   c saddest

Page 12

1. **a** I'll   **f** beach
   b aloud   **g** pear
   c eight   **h** creak
   d eye   **i** deer
   e bare

2. Cross out:
   a groan   **e** hole
   b hare   **f** Hour
   c two   **g** no
   d heard   **h** mown

Page 13

1. **a** can't   **e** I'm
   b won't   **f** I'd
   c isn't   **g** I'll
   d don't   **h** couldn't

2. **a** I'd   **e** It's
   b can't   **f** didn't
   c I'll   **g** don't

Page 14

1. **a** audition   **f** infection
   b celebration   **g** rotation
   c caution   **h** suction
   d collection   **i** hibernation
   e reflection   **j** tradition

2. **a** auction   **e** action
   b tuition   **f** fiction
   c operation   **g** exhibition
   d station

Page 15

1. **a** dog's   **e** boy's
   b girl's   **f** woman's
   c man's   **g** baby's
   d horse's

2. **a** dogs'   **e** cats'
   b girls'   **f** bats'
   c birds'   **g** boys'
   d puppies'

Page 16

1. **a** E   **d** E
   b Q   **e** E
   c Q   **f** Q

2. **a** S   **d** Q
   b E   **e** S
   c Q   **f** Q

Page 17

1. **a** I like cats, dogs and rabbits.
   b I read books, comics and newspapers.
   c My favourite foods are cake, toast and oranges.
   d I collected shells, stones and seaweed to decorate my sandcastle.
   e Rainbows are red, orange, yellow, green, blue, indigo and violet.
   f It is cold so put on a hat, scarf and gloves.
   g I drink orange juice, cola and milk.
   h I saw tigers, lions and hippos at the zoo.

2. Any sensible sentences including lists (with commas) about the subjects given.

Page 18
1. a What is your name?
   b "Can I come too?" asked Mary.
   c Why can't I? That's not fair!
   d Would you like a sweet?
   e Why not? I want to!
   f Do you like snakes?
   g Do you want to come with me? I don't mind.
   h Can we go today?
   i Who was that?
   j Would anyone like some supper?

2. a Who
   b Where
   c What
   d Why, Where or When
   e What
   f Where
   g When
   h Who
   i When or Where
   j What

Page 19
1. a cat, dog, elephant
   b cake, pie, sandwich
   c apple, orange, pear
   d baby, child, toddler
   e cup, plate, spoon

2. a Ben, Lucy, Peter
   b Jake, Nora, Selma
   c Alex, Rajan, Tom
   d Charlie, Marissa, Pat
   e Lena, Nicholas, Sophia

Page 20
1. There is no right way to segment these words; your child should break them down in any way that makes them easy to remember. Here are some suggestions:
   a sn - ail
   b writ - ing
   c ho - tel
   d may - be
   e don - key
   f flow - ers
   g car - rot
   h imp - ort - ant
   i com - put - er

2. a ou
   b oth
   c se
   d dow
   e an
   f j-ping
   g ter
   h oth - er

Page 21
1. a flew
   b laughed
   c ate
   d slid
   e roared
   f shouted
   g squeaked
   h shone
   i ran

2. a ate
   b barked
   c snores
   d wrote
   e lurked
   f galloped
   g purred
   h roared

Page 22
1. a past
   b past
   c future
   d past
   e future
   f present
   g present
   h past
   i present
   j present

2. Cross out:
   a wented
   b seen
   c saw
   d runned
   e winned
   f catched
   g seed
   h goed
   i catched

Page 23
1. a paper
   b castle
   c pot
   d bird
   e lid
   f bag
   g room
   h case
   i book
   j up

2. a scarecrow
   b skateboard
   c starfish
   d cupboard
   e haystack
   f birthday
   g bulldog
   h lipstick
   i weekend
   j football

Page 24
1. a 4
   b 1
   c 2
   d 2
   e 2
   f 3
   g 3
   h 1
   i 2
   j 2

2. a rose daisy buttercup
   b cat rabbit chinchilla
   c sun planet universe
   d eggs bacon sausages
   e lime orange banana
   f pen pencil computer
   g talk mobile telephone
   h tea coffee chocolate
   i cake trifle sandwiches
   j ant beetle scorpion

Page 25
1. a hopeful
   b joyful
   c peaceful
   d sorrowful
   e colourful
   f doubtful
   g cheerful
   h powerful
   i thoughtful

2. Any correct answers. Some suggestions are given below:
   a fabulous; a really good thing.
   b messing about in a happy way; playing games.
   c something that can be used to carry out jobs; just what is needed.
   d someone who is willing to help and make themselves useful.
   e full of hope (perhaps that something will or will not happen).
   f very happy.
   g does not lie; tells the truth.
   h lovely; attractive.
   i horrid; nasty.

Page 26
1. a kindly
   b lazily
   c happily
   d sadly
   e delicately
   f selfishly
   g roughly

2. a done with care
   b not afraid
   c shining
   d done in a lovely way
   e absolutely correct
   f fast
   g not done well
   h moving in a delicate way

Page 27
1. a basement
   b weightless
   c badness
   d endless
   e cheerfulness

2. a movement
   b bashfulness
   c enjoyment
   d agreement
   e ageless

Page 28
1. Make sure your child has learnt and can spell the words correctly.

2. Make sure your child has learnt and can spell the words correctly.

Page 29
1. a A description of main characters
   b A description of supporting characters
   c A description of where the story is set
   d A description of the weather and how it will be used to build atmosphere

2. a A good story starter
   b A description of the main event of the story
   c A description of the main problem
   d A good strong ending

Page 30
1. a Name of main character
   b Description of character
   c Description of clothes and how they might hint at the nature of the character
   d Description of character's voice
   e Description of hair/hairdo

2. a Description of the character's home
   b Description of any special habits
   c Description of character's job

Page 31
1. A 'shape' poem about a cloud, using some or all of the words in the box.
2. A list of words to use in a poem about flowers. A 'shape' poem about a flower written on the shape provided.

Page 32
1. quickly
2. slowly
3. noisily
4. often
5. never
6. nearby
7. later
8. happily
9. cheerfully
10. completely

Page 33
1. big
2. little
3. tall
4. tiny
5. long
6. golden
7. hairy
8. old
9. furry
10. brown

ANSWERS

Page 34
1. Cats drink milk.
2. Birds lay eggs.
3. The dog is asleep.
4. A balloon can pop.
5. The grass is green.
6. A frog can hop.
7. My best coat is red.
8. You swim in a pool.
9. You wash in a sink.
10. The tree is very tall.

Page 35
1. missing
2. shopping
3. writing
4. carrying
5. crashing
6. begged
7. blamed
8. copied
9. splashed
10. rubbed

Page 36
1. bit
2. broke
3. caught
4. saw
5. is
6. were
7. came
8. went
9. have
10. hurt

Page 37
1. and
2. and
3. but
4. and
5. and
6. and
7. but/and
8. but/and
9. and
10. and

Page 38
1. loud
2. down
3. mouth
4. found
5. crowd
6. clown
7. shout
8. spout
9. flower
10. crouch

Page 39
1. A farmer lives on a farm.
2. Why are you late?
3. Bees live in a hive.
4. What is the matter?
5. Where is my pen?
6. The fox ran quickly.
7. The clouds were black.
8. Who is your friend?
9. The wind is blowing.
10. How did you do it?

Page 40
1. football
2. rainbow
3. sunshine
4. snowman
5. playtime
6. butterfly
7. bulldog
8. hedgehog
9. blackberry
10. keyhole

Page 41
1. chair
2. flare
3. bear
4. cord
5. claw
6. shore
7. fire
8. cure
9. wind
10. soar

Page 42
1. The builder said, "I use a hammer."
2. The driver said, "I drive a big lorry."
3. "I am feeling tired," said Mrs Smith.
4. The librarian said, "I work in a library."
5. The farmer said, "I keep cows on my farm."
6. The queen said, "I wear a crown."
7. The nurse said, "I work in a hospital."
8. "My job is dangerous," said the firefighter.
9. The caretaker said, "I keep the school clean."
10. "I make bread," said the baker.

Page 43
1. running
2. walking
3. sitting
4. barking
5. swimming
6. flying
7. baking
8. sleeping
9. laughing
10. crying

Page 44
1. moos
2. hoots
3. clucks
4. quacks
5. gobbles
6. neighs
7. barks
8. bleats
9. squeaks
10. purrs

Page 45
1. is
2. were
3. are
4. was
5. likes
6. did
7. came
8. tore
9. tries
10. roar

Page 46
Any sensible and interesting description for each noun mentioned, to make the sentence more exciting.
e.g. The slippery green frog croaked.

Page 47
1. red, yellow, blue and green
2. lion, tiger, cheetah and leopard
3. apples, pears, bananas and grapes
4. pen, pencil, crayon and felt-tip
5. rain, sun, snow and fog
6. I saw a car, a bus, a lorry and a bike.
7. In my bag I took a mirror, a ruler and a pencil.
8. I like oranges, peaches, cherries and melons.
9. I can play football, cricket, rugby and snooker.
10. A gardener needs a spade, a fork, a trowel and a hoe.

Page 48
1. useful
2. hopeful
3. helpful
4. painful
5. beautiful
6. colour
7. faith
8. truth
9. cheer
10. plenty

Page 49
1. Who looks after our teeth?
2. What flies in the sky?
3. Where is your shirt?
4. What do we use to dig with?
5. Who lives next door to you?
6. Where do we get milk from?
7. Why are you crying?
8. How did you do that?
9. Who is your best friend?
10. What makes a seed grow?

Page 50
1. Come quickly!
2. Who are you?
3. When did you arrive?
4. Stop messing about!
5. What a nice surprise!
6. What are you doing?
7. You are horrible!
8. This cake tastes good!
9. Why are you so upset?
10. Shut that door!

Page 51
1. rabbits
2. chocolates
3. wishes
4. caps
5. ponies
6. plate
7. horse
8. box
9. rocket
10. fairy

Page 52
Answers 1–3, 4–7 and 8–9 can be given in any order.
1. January
2. June
3. July
4. September
5. October
6. November
7. December
8. April
9. August
10. February